THE EGYP

C000140745

The Egyptians created a civilization that flourished for
almost 3,000 years. Visitors to Egypt marvel at the
majestic ruins of this once-mighty kingdom: temples, pyramids, colossal statues of long-dead rulers, and their empty
tombs in the Valley of the Kings. Much has been lost to
sand and wind, and ravaged by conquest and pillage; yet
what remains is magnificently tantalizing.

An aura of mystery and magic has long surrounded the
ancient Egyptians but archaeological evidence reveals a
people who, when the gods smiled on them, enjoyed a good
life in a green land. In their cities and villages beside the
life-giving River Nile, they had as much time for fun and
games, art and music, and all the pleasures of life as they
had for the sombre rites of mummification and burial.

The tomb of Tutankhamun gives us a glimpse of the
splendours that surrounded an Egyptian pharaoh. Other
finds show everyday life: a world of bread and beer, gods
and gardens, wrestling and singing, prayers and pyramids.

*Egyptian humour: this satirical
papyrus sketch from Thebes
(c.1100 BC) shows a lion and
antelope in unlikely harmony,
playing the board game senet.*

*Egyptian majesty: the colossal head
of Ramesses II, from the temple at
Abu Simbel. The temple was moved,
piece by piece, to higher ground
(1960–68) to protect it from the
waters of the Aswan Dam project.*

*Egyptian grandeur: the temple at
Luxor floodlit at night.*

GIFT OF THE NILE

The Greek writer Herodotus, writing in the 5th century BC, called Egypt 'the gift of the Nile'. A narrow strip of green land was watered by the river, flowing north from the heart of Africa through the desert. Every year the river flooded, swollen by rains in the mountains in the south.

The people welcomed the flood, for it spread nutrient-rich black mud over their fields. Without the flood, Egypt faced famine. With it, the 'Black Land' flourished. Villagers built their homes on hillocks, surrounded by dykes and irrigation ditches, and scribes carefully recorded the Nile 'inundation' year by year, using marked stones along the river bank to check the flood level.

The rhythm of the river gave Egypt its yearly cycle and assured its people of the gods' concern. Perhaps it also explains their self-assurance. They were never afraid to tackle vast projects and their skills in engineering, medicine, astronomy and mathematics reinforced their confidence.

A wall painting from a New Kingdom tomb, depicting fishing and fowling in the Nile marshes.

The Nile at Giza, with pyramids, painted in the 1850s by Charles Theodore Frere (1814–88).

Sennedjem and his wife work their farm; from his tomb at the workers' village of Deir el-Medina, where he supervised new royal tombs in the Valley of the Kings.

The tilapia fish, a 'mouth-breeder', was a symbol of rebirth; this glass fish was found at Amarna, buried beneath the floor of a house.

Egyptian art shows people who, for the most part, look handsome and contented, drawn in elegant profile or sculpted in calm repose. Painters thought mathematically, using a grid of 18 squares to proportion the body. Sculptors thought big: no statue could be too monumental for a king. It would be hard to imagine another people who would title a book *The Correct Method of Reckoning for Understanding the Meaning of Things and Knowing Everything*.

Egyptians enjoyed life, while preparing with care for the afterlife. Families relaxed beside and on the river – boating, fishing and swimming. Noblemen dashed into the desert, in pursuit of antelope, jackal, ostrich or lion. The king rode out in his chariot to lead his army to victory against any enemy that dared defy him. And, after a 10-day working week, a favourite day out for the family was to hunt wildfowl in the marshes beside the Nile. The birds were carried home and cooked. The meal was enjoyed with wine, fruit and sweets made from honey, beneath the stars in the cool of the evening. The gods were indeed generous.

THE EGYPTIAN CALENDAR

The Egyptians had a lunar calendar for religious festivals and a solar calendar for secular events. The Egyptian year had 12 months of 30 days, with five holy days added at the end of the year, so one year had 365 days. The farmers' year had three seasons of four months: *Akhet* (flood) from July to October; *Peret* (sowing) from November to February; and *Chemu* (harvest) from March to June.

PHARAOHS AND PYRAMIDS

Imhotep, builder of the first pyramid, with a papyrus scroll. This bronze (c.600 BC) was made some 2,300 years after the architect died.

The king was elevated above other Egyptians by his parentage (his spiritual father was the sun god Ra). He was the chief priest, the link between sand and stars, and the supreme commander of the armies. From the start, the most admired kings were warriors who routed Egypt's foes.

The title 'pharaoh' (a Greek-Hebrew version of an Egyptian word meaning 'great house') was not used until fairly late in Egypt's history. Kings frequently married their sisters or half-sisters to preserve the royal bloodline. Ramesses II (c.1280 BC) had seven 'great wives', several lesser wives and a large number of concubines to ensure plenty of sons. In this regard, Ramesses was eminently successful, fathering 100 sons and 50 daughters.

Kings and queens were buried in style to guarantee their immortality: early kings built themselves pyramids; later kings chose to be interred in rock-tombs. However, neither method preserved all of the tomb treasures, intended for use in the afterlife, from the greed of thieves.

Imhotep built the first pyramid, at Saqqara, for King Djoser, and his is the first architect's name we know. His design had stepped sides. Later pyramids were faced with limestone to give a smooth, brilliant appearance. The pyramid shape had some practical advantages: it was stable and the higher it rose, the fewer stones the builders had to lift. The shape may have represented a primal sacred hill, the rays of the sun or a stairway to the stars.

THE GREAT PYRAMIDS

The three 'great pyramids' at Giza were built for Khufu, his son Khafre and Menkaure, who was probably Khafre's brother. The Great Pyramid, built for Khufu, is the largest, at 147 metres (482 feet) tall. It was made of an estimated 2.5 million blocks of limestone, with an average weight of 2.5 tons. Khafre's, while 3 metres (10 feet) lower, is on higher ground. The three pyramids were surrounded by avenues of smaller tombs for the royal family and courtiers.

Narmer, the 1st-Dynasty king (c.3100 BC), is depicted holding a beaten enemy by the hair and about to kill him with a mace.

Seti I, ruler from 1318–1304 BC and father of Ramesses II; from his tomb, the most splendid in the Valley of the Kings.

Care was taken to select a site on firm rock and to align the pyramid entrance to face north, using the pole star as a marker. Herodotus, visiting Egypt in the 5th century BC, more than 2,000 years after the Great Pyramid of Khufu was built, calculated a workforce of 100,000; modern estimates are around 20,000. It probably took between 10 and 20 years to complete the job.

BUILDING TO THE STARS

A wall painting showing Egyptian tomb-workers hauling stones with ropes.

The pyramid-builders, mostly farmers, arrived on the building site each year in late summer, after the harvest had been gathered and the Nile flood had made farm work impossible. They joined a skeleton crew of workers who were on site all year. Pyramid-builders were not slaves, although foreign prisoners of war may have been used as forced labour. They were paid in bread (10 loaves a day) and worked in teams of 200; some left their names scrawled in red paint on blocks of stone. One team called itself 'Menkaure's drunks'.

Astonishing feats of construction were performed with hardly any machinery. The builders cut huge limestone blocks from quarries using stone tools, and wooden wedges soaked with water to make the wood expand and the stone split more readily. Stones were dragged to the site on wooden sledges. Watering the sand reduced friction, so a dozen men could shift a block weighing up to 2 tons. The biggest stones were 150 times heavier. How stones were raised into position as the pyramid rose higher remains something of a mystery, although it is likely they were hauled up ramps, using ropes and the muscles of hundreds of men.

The Sphinx, eroded by wind and sand, and still mysterious, gazes out beyond the Great Pyramid at Giza.

Most pyramids are geometrically remarkably accurate. Deep inside the pyramid, workers constructed the royal burial chamber and inserted a stone sarcophagus, as yet empty. The finished pyramid stood empty until the king died. After a splendid funeral, his mummified body was entombed in a chamber decorated with wall paintings, and surrounded by treasures, domestic items, food and drink for his use in the next world. The priests left, having put the final magic symbols in the tomb to avert evil, and the last workers scrambled out, sealing the claustrophobic passageway behind them.

In spite of the ingenuity, the spells, dummy tunnels and blocked entrances, every pyramid was broken into and some or all of its contents stolen within 200 years of completion. Tomb robbers were not deterred by superstitious fears or by the prospect of being trapped if a tunnel collapsed.

PYRAMID PUZZLES

Eccentric theories surround the pyramids – that they are sundials or giant geometric puzzles, or that they foretell the future. There are strange theories about extraterrestrial visitors as well as claims that a pyramid can sharpen a blunt razor blade. Napoleon entered the Great Pyramid in 1799 and came out looking pale and shaken, although he never told anyone why.

Workers at rest; the tomb-builders lived on site close to the pyramids. This is the workers' cemetery, with a miniature pyramid.

The Battle of the Pyramids (1798), when Napoleon defeated the Mamelukes in Egypt; painting by Louis Lejeune (1775–1848).

LIFE AS AN EGYPTIAN

Counting livestock. This painted wood model shows Egyptian civil servants doing what they were best at – list-making.

The head of a princess from the family of Akhenaten, New Kingdom.

Egyptian society was itself pyramidal. At the top was the king, the link between people and the gods. His vizier (chief official), army commanders and provincial governors carried out his orders. Priests and scribes saw to the everyday conduct of religious and civil affairs, skilled workers from doctors to weavers plied their trades, and farmers ploughed, sowed and harvested.

Women in Egypt could own land and run businesses, such as weaving shops and bakeries, as well as having traditional female roles as midwives and mourners. Nebet, the wife of a nomarch (provincial governor) in the 6th Dynasty, rose to become a magistrate and judge. On the tomb of Pesheshet, who lived in the 5th Dynasty, it is recorded that she was 'overseer of the physicians'. Some queens had considerable power: Hatshepsut ruled in her own right as pharaoh from 1503 to 1482 BC, assuming the full regalia (including a false beard).

Women usually married between the ages of 13 and 15 and could expect to be grandmothers by the age of 30. Registers of citizens, like that for the tomb-workers' village at Deir el-Medina, list occupants of homes, but there are no references to a religious marriage ceremony. Husbands made gifts to their brides and were also expected to be generous to a divorced wife.

Children were regarded as essential to a successful marriage: small fertility symbols are often found in house-shrines and in tombs, and were probably given as presents to childless couples. Adoption was common. Pregnant women sought divine aid from the goddess Taweret, who had the body of a hippo and the legs of a lion, and wore a crocodile-tail headdress. Bes, the merry dwarf god, and Heket, the frog goddess, might also intercede to bring an easy and successful birth. If a husband died before his wife, his wife inherited two-thirds of the estate, the rest going to his brothers and his children.

Most boys in ancient Egypt learned their fathers' trades, while girls were taught domestic arts at home. The well-to-do paid for private tutors or sent boys to school. Schoolchildren wrote on fragments of pottery or limestone, which were much cheaper than papyrus. School was a serious business. Boys who ran away from school had wooden blocks tied to their ankles.

Monarch of all. The magnificent gold funerary mask of Tutankhamun bears the emblem of the vulture, symbol of his rule over Upper Egypt, and the cobra for Lower Egypt.

RUNNING THE KINGDOM

With so many important sacred duties, the pharaoh delegated much routine business to his vizier. In the New Kingdom, there were three such 'prime ministers', who shared administrative duties in the three regions: Lower Egypt, Upper Egypt and the South (Nubia). The viziers, chosen from the best scribes in the land, were the eyes and ears of the pharaohs. For local government, Egypt was split into 42 provincial districts, each with its own capital, army and governor.

Queen Nefertari, 'Great Royal Wife' of Ramesses II, playing the board game senet.

THE EGYPTIAN LOOK

In the searing heat, Egyptian clothing was cool, light and airy, and often scanty. Men wore short skirts, like kilts, stripping to loincloths for manual work; women wore dresses, court women shimmering about in clinging garments made of linen and often beautifully embroidered. Sheep's wool was worn only as an over-garment, not touching the skin. Children often wore no clothes at all. Most Egyptians went barefoot or wore sandals made from plaited reeds, palm leaves or grass, with leather sandals for special occasions.

Both men and women wore wigs made from human hair, wool or palm fibres. Wigs were symbols of status and also protected against insects and the sun. On a hot night, women attending a banquet wore cones of fat or wax mixed with perfume on top of their wigs. As the cone melted slowly, cooling perfume oozed over the wearer. Priests shaved their heads and never wore wigs. Young boys also had shaven heads, except for one plaited lock, which was cut off when they reached manhood. Black was the preferred hair colour. Greying hair was dyed: a preparation made from the blood of a black calf or black cat might do the trick if one could not get the fat of a black snake or gazelle.

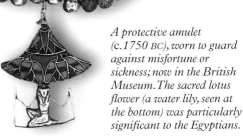

A protective amulet (c.1750 BC), worn to guard against misfortune or sickness; now in the British Museum. The sacred lotus flower (a water lily, seen at the bottom) was particularly significant to the Egyptians.

Ptahkhenuwy and his wife, two painted limestone figurines from an Old Kingdom tomb at Giza.

Eye makeup was used by men and women. Often, a heavy black line would be applied to the upper lid, using kohl from galena or lead ore, while a green shadow, from malachite, would be used on the lower. Rich women carried their makeup boxes with them to parties, to refresh the paintwork as required. Mirrors of polished copper were shaped like flowers, animals or the *ankh* symbol of eternal life.

Jewellery was worn by both men and women, for magical as well as aesthetic reasons: for example, a fish pendant might protect a child from drowning and an amulet in the form of a god would draw down divine protection. A favourite stone was lapis lazuli, its blue colour reminding people of the sky. Tutankhamun had many amulet 'lucky charms' inside his mummy wrappings and he was buried wearing 13 bracelets on his arms. People often wore two or three rings on the same finger. Gold represented the flesh of the sun god Ra, although silver, rare in Egypt, was even more prized.

Some of the most impressive Egyptian jewellery pieces were pectorals (chest ornaments) and jewelled collars made of metal, glass, stone or faience (steatite or clay with crushed quartz, overlaid with coloured glass). Most magnificent of all was the royal crown, crafted in gold and semi-precious stones, surmounted by the sacred *uraeus* cobra, the snake that symbolically protected the king and spat defiance at his enemies.

A mirror case in the form of an ankh, *from the tomb of Tutankhamun; made of wood, gilded and inlaid with glass paste, it bears the king's name flanked by lotus flowers.*

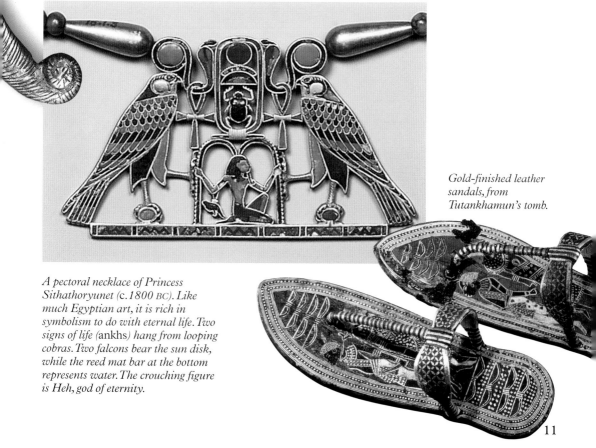

Gold-finished leather sandals, from Tutankhamun's tomb.

*A pectoral necklace of Princess Sithathoryunet (c.1800 BC). Like much Egyptian art, it is rich in symbolism to do with eternal life. Two signs of life (*ankhs*) hang from looping cobras. Two falcons bear the sun disk, while the reed mat bar at the bottom represents water. The crouching figure is Heh, god of eternity.*

11

DOMESTIC LIFE

While Egypt's masses huddled in cramped cottages, the better-off had two-storey houses with small gardens, and court officials spread themselves in 30-room mansions, decorated with elegant murals and woven hangings. Humbler citizens used their front rooms as shops or workshops and kept goats or geese there at night.

Small clay-model houses were put in tombs, giving us a fairly accurate idea of what small homes looked like. A typical worker's house had mud-brick walls. Made from Nile mud mixed with straw and sand, moulded and baked in the sun for two or three days, mud-bricks were cheap and plentiful, but if there was heavy rainfall or a Nile flood that was higher than usual, much repair and rebuilding of crumbling buildings was necessary. Fired bricks were used from about 1900 BC for steps and floors.

Two women enjoy the music of a harpist, from a painter's tomb at the workers' village of Deir el-Medina.

A wooden model of a servant girl carrying bread and meat home in her basket (c.1900 BC).

Timber was scarce, but it was in high demand for making doors, windows and furniture. Flat roofs were made of palm logs covered over with mud plaster. A scoop-like ventilator on the roof caught the breeze, to relieve the heat inside. Floors were of hard-packed earth, with reed mats on top, although the rich walked on tiles made of gypsum or bricks laid on mud plaster. The stairs were outside and the kitchen often separate in a small, walled enclosure. Large houses had outbuildings for servants and for domestic tasks such as baking and weaving. In the garden were flowers, vegetables, palm and fruit trees, grape vines and ponds.

The tomb-workers' village at Deir el-Medina. Mud-brick houses, with plastered walls and flat roofs, were built close together. The front doors opened on to the street.

Windows were small and set high, usually on two sides of a room so that a cooling breeze could blow through, and with woven matting blinds. Jars of water, vases of flowers and oil lamps rested on elegant wooden stands. The lamps were made from hollowed stone, pottery or alabaster.

Furnishings were sparse, mainly because wood was so scarce. Poor people sat on stools or mats. Chairs had leather-strap seats and carved legs; dining tables were small. The tomb of Khufu's mother, Queen Hetepheres, discovered at Giza in 1925, contained a wooden bed, two armchairs and a linen chest. The furniture makers used the same joints as we do today (dovetail, mortice and tenon). Beds were sprung with straps and cords. Sheets were made of linen; there were no pillows, the sleeper resting his or her cheek on a shallow U-shaped rest.

Tutankhamun's ivory headrest. Ordinary people had rather less elegant bedroom furniture.

While most people bathed in the river or in the nearest irrigation ditch, the rich had small bathrooms. They bathed with the aid of a servant, who tipped water over them. Many homes had a toilet, or rather a sand closet. Closets may have connected to a cesspit, with the waste later dug out, sun-dried and used on the fields as manure. Street refuse was scavenged by vultures and kites.

SCRIBES AND WARRIOR KINGS

There were many jobs an Egyptian boy might aspire to but an ambitious student might choose to become a scribe. Would-be scribes toiling at school were, no doubt, encouraged by a teacher's reminder that many other jobs were worse: coppersmiths suffered burns, boatmen might be devoured by crocodiles, and builders might be crushed by stones.

A scribe had to master at least 700 hieroglyphs or picture-signs (used for religious texts – simpler writing was used for day-to-day matters), but he paid no taxes and was excused from manual labour. Writing busily on papyrus scrolls or wax tablets, or (most formally) inscribing walls, he was clerk, manager and historian. He kept records of food supplies, taxes, livestock, construction projects, army stores and the Nile floods, as well as describing for posterity events such as foreign expeditions and the king's victories over Egypt's enemies. After a battle, the hands of dead enemies were chopped off, counted, and the number recorded by scribes.

Stone tablet showing four scribes busily at work (c.1400 BC).

REEDS FOR READING

Papyrus is a tall reed-like water plant. The Egyptians made 'paper' from its stems, which they cut into strips, and then pressed in layers to form matted sheets. The process of making papyrus was a state secret until the 1st century BC.

On the march. These model soldiers dating from c.2000 BC, carry the hide-covered shields and spears that were standard kit for the pharaohs' armies.

While many images show 'barbarians' slain by a rampant pharaoh, or bound as captives, at first the Egyptians at war were less well equipped than their opponents, fighting on foot with wooden spears and feeble bows. Improvements were effected by General Wemi in the reign of Pepy I (6th Dynasty), and by 2500 BC the army was kitted out with axes, copper daggers and leather armour. Copper was mined in the desert and was the principal metal, although bronze (copper alloyed with tin) was harder. Iron, which the Egyptians called 'metal from heaven', was unknown until relatively late in their history: a Hittite king sent Ramesses II an iron sword as a gift in about 1300 BC.

Egyptian weapons were made of copper or bronze. Soldiers also used stone maces, as clubs, as well as small axes.

Military decorations included the Golden Fly, and among the recipients was Queen Aahotep I, whose husband was killed fighting the Hyksos, or 'Shepherd Kings', who invaded northern Egypt in about 1630 BC. Their weaponry included the horse-chariot and composite bow, soon adopted by the Egyptians. To defend their territory, notably in the south, the Egyptians built large forts, such as Buhen and Semna, with mud-brick walls 40 metres (130 feet) high. When campaigning abroad, they became proficient, and patient, in siege warfare – the siege of Ashdod (Israel) in the 600s BC lasted 29 years.

In boats like this, a tomb model, soldiers went up and down the Nile to man Egypt's forts and subdue its enemies; now in the Ashmolean Museum, Oxford.

TEMPLES AND PALACES

Along the banks of the Nile were magnificent temples and palaces. Temples, like pyramids, were built with the heavens in mind: their roofs served as stellar observatories for priest-astronomers. Over time, the temple evolved from a simple mud-brick structure to a massive edifice, with immense stone columns decorated with papyrus, palm and lotus designs, supporting a stone roof.

The entrance was through a pylon, or ceremonial gateway, aligned so that the sun rose and set between its vertical pillars. In many temples, the sun's rays shone directly through into the sanctuary that housed the god's statue. A priests' daily routine included washing the statue and presenting three meals a day to the god. He would then eat the food himself in lieu of wages. Temple estates employed many people; their buildings would have included priestly accommodation, a school, workshops, a granary and storehouses.

Probably the biggest temple ever built, the temple of Amun-Ra at Karnak, near the city of Luxor, covered 2 hectares (5 acres). This view shows the sacred lake where priests bathed to purify themselves.

The temple at Karnak, constantly enriched and enlarged, attained the status of a national monument. Its high priest managed huge revenues from its estates and from booty brought back by Egypt's victorious armies. One of its most striking features is the hypostyle ('pillared roof') hall, 100 metres (330 feet) long, containing 134 columns, the 12 tallest of which are 21 metres (70 feet) high. The temple must have been staggering in its prime and retains an immense aura. There are 24-metre (80-foot) obelisks set up by Tuthmosis I (*c.*1525–1512 BC) and Queen Hatshepsut. An even larger obelisk erected at Karnak by Tuthmosis III is now in Rome; 32 metres (105 feet) high and weighing around 230 tons, it is the biggest Egyptian obelisk to survive.

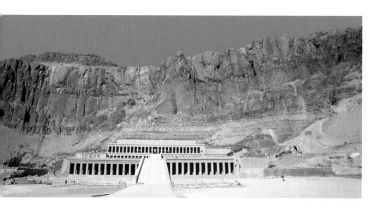

The mortuary temple of Hatshepsut at Deir el-Bahri. Defaced by her successor, it was reduced to rubble by the AD 1800s, but has been reconstructed to recreate its stunning colonnades.

Little remains of once-spectacular Egyptian royal palaces. Pictures in royal tombs offer glimpses of their elegance, with walls painted in soothing colours and scenes of wildlife and plants. One of the most striking was built for Akhenaten (Amenhotep IV), who in the 1300s BC moved his court out of Thebes to his new city, Akhetaten. Its ruins are today visible at the small town of Amarna. This was probably where the young Tutankhamun (most likely the son or brother of Akhenaten) grew up. There were two palaces: a great palace for ceremonial, and another for the king's family, with a private zoo and a boating lake.

The temple at Karnak has six gateways, or pylons. This avenue of ram's-head sphinxes (representing the sun god Ra) led to the first pylon. A second avenue is over 3 kilometres (2 miles) long and had 1,400 human-headed sphinxes.

Cleopatra's Needle, erected by Tuthmosis III about 1500 BC, was given to Britain by the viceroy of Egypt in 1819. It has stood on the Thames Embankment in London since it arrived in 1878. Its twin is in Central Park, New York.

OBELISKS

Egyptian obelisks may have been a fertility symbol as well as a tribute to the sun. They tapered at the top to a small pyramid shape or pyramidion, said to symbolize the primeval hill or *ben-ben* from which all life originated. Obelisks were probably raised by first dragging them up a ramp, then tilting them vertically into an enclosed sandpit from which the sand was slowly removed to let the obelisk sink into position. An inscription on Hatshepsut's obelisk at Karnak suggests it took seven months to quarry the stone.

EMPIRE OF THE GODS

King Khafre, protected by Horus. This life-size figure of the pyramid-king is made of grained diorite (a crystalline rock). All kings regarded themselves as re-embodiments of the god Horus.

E gypt had a colourful pantheon of gods. Every city had its own protector god, and over time, gods formed families, or merged with other deities. The Egyptians believed that the world had begun in a dark ocean, from which arose a hill and the creator god Atum, who later took on another identity as Ra, the sun god.

Alum coughed from his mouth air (Shu) and moisture (Tefnut). Shu parted the earth (Geb) and the sky (Nut) to produce five children: Osiris, Isis, Horus, Nepthys and Seth. Osiris and Isis had a son, also named Horus; Nepthys also had a son, Anubis, the jackal-headed god of death. The most feared god was Seth, spirit of the hostile desert.

The sky god Amun, originally the protector god of Thebes and often shown with a ram's head, was later declared to be Ra in another form. As Amun-Ra, he became Egypt's national god. Every king called himself the son of Ra, but all Egyptians identified with Osiris, god of the afterlife.

Osiris gave Egypt its civilization, teaching people agriculture, art and government. His wife, Isis, taught domestic skills such as spinning and weaving, watched over marriages and could cure sickness with her magic charms. Isis was much loved, for she had restored Osiris to life after his murder and mutilation by his brother Seth.

A god, his wife and child formed a triad. Here are Osiris, the resurrected and resurrector (centre), with his wife Isis, the mother-goddess, and their son Horus.

The entrance to the temple at Edfu; the pylon stands 36 metres (118 feet) high and is inscribed with images of two late-period kings, Ptolemy III and Ptolemy IV.

The lion-headed Sekhmet, a goddess whose wrath was frightful and whose appetite for flesh was ravenous.

There were many other deities, some with animal attributes: Hathor, often depicted as a woman wearing cow's horns, was the goddess of love, beauty and the pleasures of life; Thoth, the god of wisdom, had the head of an ibis (and sometimes a baboon); the jackal-headed Anubis presided over funeral rites and led the dead to judgement before Osiris; and Sekhmet was a fearsome lion-headed goddess.

The pharaoh maintained the balance between the world of humans and the world of the gods. This balance was called *ma'at*, and in time Ma'at became the goddess of truth, balance and order. The pharaoh went to a temple every day. Ordinary people said their prayers at home and never set foot inside a temple's inner sanctuary. During a god's special festival, the god-statue would be brought out for all to see. When a person died, rituals ensured that they would cross safely from the human world to the world of the gods.

Egypt's ancient cults survived until 'paganism' was banned by the Roman emperor in AD 391. Coptic Christianity triumphed and the last great symbol of the old gods, the Temple of Isis at Philae, was closed in AD 551. The arrival of Islam in the 600s completed the transformation.

19

MUMMIFICATION AND THE AFTERLIFE

The Egyptians believed that every person was made up of five different aspects: a name (*ren*), given to them at birth; a spiritual double or soul (*ka*); a life force (*ba*, often shown as a bird); a 'shining form' (*akh*); and a shadow (*sheut*). For successful rebirth into the afterlife, all these aspects had to be reunited with an intact body. That is why Egyptians took such pains to preserve the body, as a mummy.

The 'first-class' process of mummification (there were cheaper alternatives) took at least 70 days, starting with the removal of the intestines, stomach, lungs and liver. These were preserved in four 'canopic jars'. The brain, not valued in the afterlife, was extracted from the skull through the nose. The heart was left, since in the next world it would be weighed against a feather to determine whether the person would join the afterlife: if the heart was heavier than the feather, being weighed down with sins committed during life, a devouring monster condemned it and the person to oblivion; if the heart was lighter than the feather, the person would enter the next world.

Weighing the heart against a feather: Anubis weighs, Thoth records and Horus watches.

The mummy case of a priest named Ankh Hor; now in Norwich Castle Museum.

Tomb models of carpenters at work (c.2000 BC). Many tools used by Egyptians closely resembled those still in use today.

ENSURING A LONG RETIREMENT

If you had to work for the king in life, you might have to work for the gods in the afterlife. So people had *shabti* – small figurines of servants or labourers – placed in their tombs. They believed the figures would come to life in the next world and work for them, carrying out any menial tasks that the gods might require.

The body was packed with natural salt (natron, from a dry lake), and left for 40 days. When dried out, the cavity was stuffed with linen, the incision stitched up, and wads of linen, onions or white stone 'eyes' placed in the eye sockets. The body was wrapped in linen cloth. Protective amulets and flowers were bandaged in and often a winged scarab was placed with the body. Khephri or Khephre, the scarab beetle god, was associated with Ra, and the scarab was a popular amulet connected to the idea of rebirth. When it had been wrapped, the mummy was painted with oils and perfumes, and a mask was put on its face. After the funeral, the mummy was removed from its coffin and placed upright, while priests performed the 'opening of the mouth' ceremony to prepare the body for its journey. It was then placed in its coffin or coffins (kings having several, one within the other).

Rulers of the 18th and 20th Dynasties were buried in rock-tombs in the Valley of the Kings. Each tomb was entered by a long passage, opening into a funeral chamber. The walls were painted with scenes from life and sacred texts. Hieroglyphs, now known as the 'Book of the Dead', containing up to 200 spells, were written on papyrus scrolls and rolled up inside wooden statues in the tomb.

The limestone sarcophagus of Seti I; now in Sir John Soane's Museum, London.

Burial mask (c.1900 BC) from the mummy of an official named Ankhef. He was at least 45 when he died, and suffered from osteoarthritis in his spine. The mask was made of moulded linen stiffened with plaster. It showed the face of the deceased, golden-skinned as in the afterlife.

AT HOME AND ABROAD

The Nile was Egypt's thoroughfare for everything from grain to obelisks. The Egyptians built sailing craft as early as 3000 BC and ventured abroad into the Red Sea and the eastern Mediterranean, trading with Crete, Greece, Syria and Byblos (Lebanon), where African ebony might be exchanged for cedar and cypress wood. Boats played a ceremonial part in royal funerals. Khufu's funeral boat, discovered in 1954, was in 1,000 marked sections and is 43 metres (140 feet) long.

Around 2280 BC, a royal official named Harkhuf journeyed south into Nubia and the Sudan, returning with 300 asses laden with incense, ivory and animal skins; a second trip produced an even more interesting item, a 'dancing pygmy', much to the delight of the young pharaoh, Pepy I. Eight hundred years later, Queen Hatshepsut sent a seaborne expedition to Punt (probably Somalia), recorded on the walls of her mortuary temple at Deir el-Bahri. Among its prizes were giraffe skins, live baboons and myrrh trees, planted in the temple garden.

SHOPPING WITHOUT CASH

No coins were used in ancient Egypt. While Egyptians believed everything belonged to the pharoah, they also bought and sold by bartering. A standard weight of copper, the *deben* (about 85 grams/ 3 ounces), represented an agreed value during a transaction. Later (c.500 BC) Egyptians used metal rings as tokens.

Exotic animals brought back by trading expeditions were a source of fascination, but lions were more familiar. This workman's sketch, on limestone, shows a lion's head, with fleeing quail chicks.

An Egyptian sailing vessel, with oars for steering and propulsion, as well as a sail. Being short of timber, the Egyptians built vessels from bundles of reeds as well as planks.

A traveller returning from such an expedition would have much to tell and gifts to display, perhaps at a banquet with the king himself or with his family. At an Egyptian dinner, raw cabbage was served as an appetizer, in the belief that it increased the thirst for wine – made in red, white and rosé. Beer was the staple drink of workers. At an annual beer festival, drinkers sampled a brew coloured with red ochre, recalling the story of how the god Ra calmed the carnivorous goddess Sekhmet by getting her tipsy on red beer, which she thought was blood.

Maringa oil, garlic and onions played an important part in Egyptian cookery. Lettuce was believed to be an aphrodisiac, while honey was used as a sweetener, along with dates and fruit juice. Egyptian bread was very gritty, because sand got into flour when it was milled. The result was heavy wear on the teeth and plenty of dental problems. People ate lamb and beef, even though the goddess Hathor was bovine, and lots of fish, although fish were shunned by priests as 'unclean'. People ate with their fingers; it was polite to use only the thumb, index finger and middle finger.

The grape harvest in full swing: the Egyptians enjoyed wine with dinner, though poorer folk usually drank beer; from the tomb of a scribe at Thebes.

A heavenly feast in prospect: this Old Kingdom relief (c.2330 BC) shows servants carrying a haunch of beef and a duck; from the tomb of Princess Idut.

A CATALOGUE OF GLORIES

The New Kingdom's 18th Dynasty saw several mighty rulers: Amenhotep I, Tuthmosis I, Hatshepsut and Tuthmosis III – the greatest of the soldier-kings, who brought Palestine and Syria into his empire. There was a short-lived cultural revolution in the reign of Amenhotep IV (1353–36 BC). This remarkable ruler introduced a new religion based on the worship of one god, the sun god or Aten. He took a new name, Akhenaten ('one useful to Aten'), built a new capital city, Akhetaten, and encouraged a new wave of artistic expression.

Tutankhamun and his wife, Ankhesenpaten. He was married at the age of nine; she was the daughter of Akhenaten, and possibly Tutankhamun's half-sister. Two children were still-born, and later buried with the king.

A bust of Queen Nefertiti, dating from c.1360 BC. She was the most important of Akhenaten's two wives, and helped plan his new city of Akhetaten (Amarna).

This elegant gold piece, from the tomb of Tutankhamun and now in the Egyptian National Museum, Cairo, shows the king's triumphant return with prisoners.

ALEXANDRIA

The Library at Alexandria was the biggest in the ancient world, with 400,000 manuscripts. The city's towering lighthouse was one of the Seven Wonders of the Ancient World, and a 'must-see' for tourists, after the pyramids.

This was heresy to the Egyptian establishment. Akhenaten's reign ended with the restoration of the old cults and when in 1333 Tutankhaten came to the throne he changed his name to Tutankhamun to demonstrate his allegiance to the old ways and the old god Amun-Ra. Horemheb, the last king of the 18th Dynasty, restored religious pluralism and, under the strong 19th-Dynasty kings, including Seti I and Ramesses II, Egypt seemed as secure as ever.

The decline began from the 20th Dynasty onwards. The country fragmented. Short-lived dynasties came and went, and foreigners took control: there were Nubian, Assyrian and Persian rulers. Persian rule was ended in 332 BC by Alexander the Great of Macedonia, who founded the city of Alexandria and the dynasty of the Ptolemies. Alexander was crowned as a pharaoh and made sacrifices to the gods. He died in Babylon, aged almost 33, reportedly having become ill after a drinking party. His body is said to have been returned to Alexandria for burial.

Cleopatra, last of the great rulers, was a Ptolemy. She became queen in 51 BC at the age of 18. Her affair with Julius Caesar in 46 BC included a spectacular cruise along the Nile and produced a son, Cesarion. Rumour accused her of poisoning her younger brother to make sure Cesarion inherited her throne. A second Roman affair, with Mark Antony, produced a son and two daughters. After defeat at the Battle of Actium, and Antony's suicide, Cleopatra tried to win over Rome's new leader, Octavian (later Emperor Augustus). But he resisted her charms and, rather than face the humiliation of becoming his trophy-captive, she killed herself.

Egypt was absorbed into the Roman Empire. The Romans catalogued Egypt's treasures, took away what they liked, and the sands began to drift over the temples and tombs.

Limestone head, thought to be of Cleopatra. Her children with Antony were brought up in Rome by his ex-wife Octavia. Cesarion, son of Julius Caesar, was strangled, to eliminate him as a claimant to the throne of either Egypt or Rome.

THE EGYPTOLOGISTS

Howard Carter examines the mummified remains of Tutankhamun. Many thousands of mummies must have been made, but only around 1,000 survive.

Is this the face of Tutankhamun? Based on forensic evidence and CT scans of his remains, it bears a marked resemblance to known images of the king, who died aged 19, possibly after suffering a knee injury that led to blood poisoning.

When the Greek traveller Strabo visited Egypt in 25 BC, he found many sites abandoned and vanishing under the encroaching sand. The Romans treated Egypt like an antiques warehouse, removing statues and obelisks: Rome today has over twice as many obelisks as there are in Egypt.

Interest in Egypt remained mercenary for many centuries. The Caliph al-Ma'mun smashed his way into the Great Pyramid in the 800s with a battering ram. Europeans knew of the pyramids from travellers' tales, but few had seen them. In the 16th century John Sanderson brought back quantities of mummies to England, and in 1639 Oxford mathematician John Greaves and his party crawled 'serpent-like … on our bellies' to explore the pyramids. All he found were scorpions and bats, but he did make the first scientific measurements of the pyramids.

Collectors began to acquire Egyptian artefacts. When Sir Hans Sloane died in 1753, his collection, including some 150 objects from Egypt, became the foundation of the British Museum. Travellers began visiting Egypt as part of the 'grand tour', though Richard Pococke in 1737 was alarmed to see temple columns being cut up for millstones.

Popular interest in Egypt was spurred by the enthralling search for the source of the Nile by Victorian explorers, and by the exploits of travellers such as Lady Lucie Duff-Gordon, who lived for six years on top of the temple at Luxor (by then almost covered by sand) until her death in 1869. The great era of Egyptology began with Giovanni Belzoni, a former showground strongman who became an indefatigable burrower into buried temples and pyramids, while artists such as David Roberts (1796–1864) painted Egyptian splendours. There was a wave of interest in Egyptian design, archaeology and mysticism, and a new scholarly enthusiasm following the cracking of the previously unreadable hieroglyphs.

Probably the greatest name in Egyptian archaeology is Sir Flinders Petrie (1853–1942), who began work at Giza in 1880. His strengths were his careful recording of excavations and his interest in everyday objects. The tomb of Tutankhamun, found in 1922 and opened the next year, made a celebrity of one of Petrie's former students, Howard Carter, and put ancient Egypt on the front pages of every newspaper.

The Rosetta Stone, which unlocked the door to the secret world of Egyptian hieroglyphs.

CRACKING THE CODE

The Egyptian writing system caused excitement and bafflement in equal measure, since no one could read hieroglyphs. In 1799 the French found a basalt slab at Rosetta bearing what appeared to be the same inscription in three different scripts: hieroglyphs (1,419 signs), cursive demotic (a late version of spoken Egyptian) and 486 words of Greek. French scholar Jean-François Champollion toiled for more than 20 years before he finally deciphered the hieroglyphs, so opening new avenues in Egyptian studies.

Sarcophagus lid of Ramesses II. Antiquities like this were brought back to Europe and acquired by collectors, such as Richard, 7th Viscount Fitzwilliam. The Cambridge museum bearing his name, founded in 1816, now houses this and other Egyptian treasures.

LEGACY OF THE PHARAOHS

Archaeology is now a disciplined science, far removed from the treasure-hunting days, but people's fascination with Egypt has remained undimmed. Egypt's monuments and museum relics remain awe-inspiring. Egypt also retains much of its mystique, amid the usually wildly inaccurate exploitation of Egyptian mummies and mysticism in Hollywood films, computer games and children's cartoons.

Egyptian art and architecture has become a powerful influence on modern creativity. The glass pyramid in front of the Louvre Museum in Paris is an elegant architectural example, but the pyramid pops up in many other guises, from Victorian cemeteries to hotels in Las Vegas.

Museum collections have played a vital role in conserving the relics of Egypt's grandeur. Many of the finds now displayed in museums were retrieved by amateur collectors, while others are the product of painstaking work by archaeologists. The Egyptian galleries at the British Museum and Sir John Soane's Museum in London, the Fitzwilliam in Cambridge, the Ashmolean in Oxford, and Norwich Castle Museum (to name but five) contain priceless objects. No museum has more impressive evidence of Egypt's riches than the Egyptian Museum in Cairo, which proudly houses the treasures of Tutankhamun.

Millions of tourists visit Egypt to see for themselves. The magic remains and the Nile still flows – although, since the construction in the 1960s of the Aswan Dam, it no longer floods uncontrolled as it did in the time of the pharaohs.

Ages-old style can still attract the modern eye, as in these pieces of jewellery, which draw their inspiration from Egypt.

A sphinx in London, beside Cleopatra's Needle. The bronze sphinxes flanking the obelisk on the Thames Embankment date from the 1870s, and reflect Victorian artists' interest in all things Egyptian.

The Valley of the Kings – a magnet for tourists and still a place that draws archaeologists and scientists, keen to uncover more hidden secrets.